K

Ready for School

Written by Hanna Otero

Illustrations by Heidi Chang

FlashKids

An imprint of Sterling Children's Books

This book belongs to

_____

FLASH KIDS, STERLING, and the distinctive Sterling logo are registered trademarks of
Sterling Publishing Co., Inc.

Published by Sterling Publishing Co., Inc.
387 Park Avenue South, New York, NY 10016
Text and illustrations © 2006 by Flash Kids
Distributed in Canada by Sterling Publishing
c/o Canadian Manda Group, 165 Dufferin Street
Toronto, Ontario, Canada M6K 3H6
Distributed in the United Kingdom by GMC Distribution Services
Castle Place, 166 High Street, Lewes, East Sussex, England BN7 1XU
Distributed in Australia by Capricorn Link (Australia) Pty. Ltd.
P.O. Box 704, Windsor, NSW 2756, Australia

Sterling ISBN 978-1-4114-3466-0

Manufactured in Canada

Lot #:
10 12 14 15 13 11
04/13

For information about custom editions, special sales, premium and
corporate purchases, please contact Sterling Special Sales
Department at 800-805-5489 or specialsales@sterlingpublishing.com.

Cover design and production by Mada Design, Inc.

Dear Parent,

Starting school is an important and exciting event for any child. *Ready for School* will help your child develop the skills he or she needs to excel in the classroom. The book introduces basic number activities, plus practice in matching, sequencing, patterns, and letter sounds. These basic skills will build the foundation for reading and math. To get the most from this book, follow these simple steps:

- Find a comfortable place where you and your child can work quietly together.
- Encourage your child to go at his or her own pace.
- Help your child sound out the letters and identify the pictures.
- Offer lots of praise and support.
- Let your child reward his or her work with the included stickers.
- Most of all, remember that learning should be fun! Take time to color the pictures, laugh at the funny characters, and enjoy this special time spent together.

Colors

Color each food. Trace the name of the color.

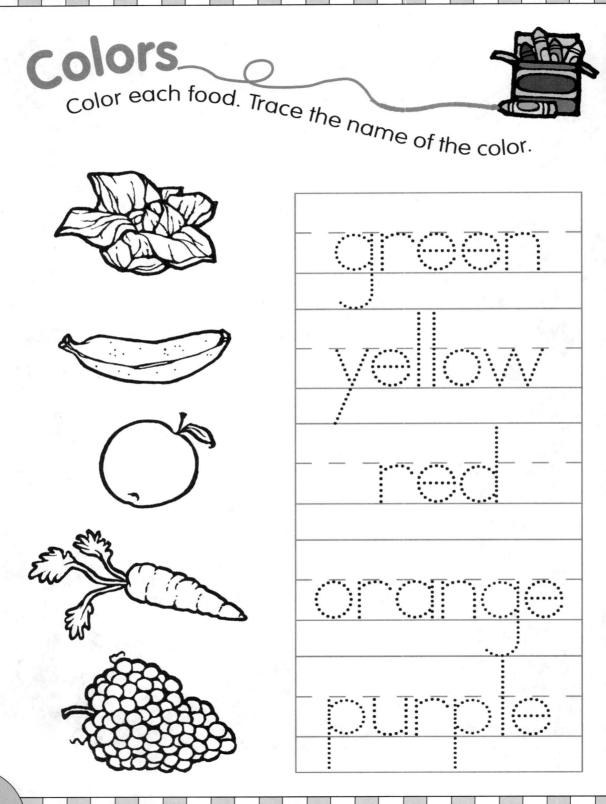

green

yellow

red

orange

purple

More Colors

Color each animal. Trace the name of the color.

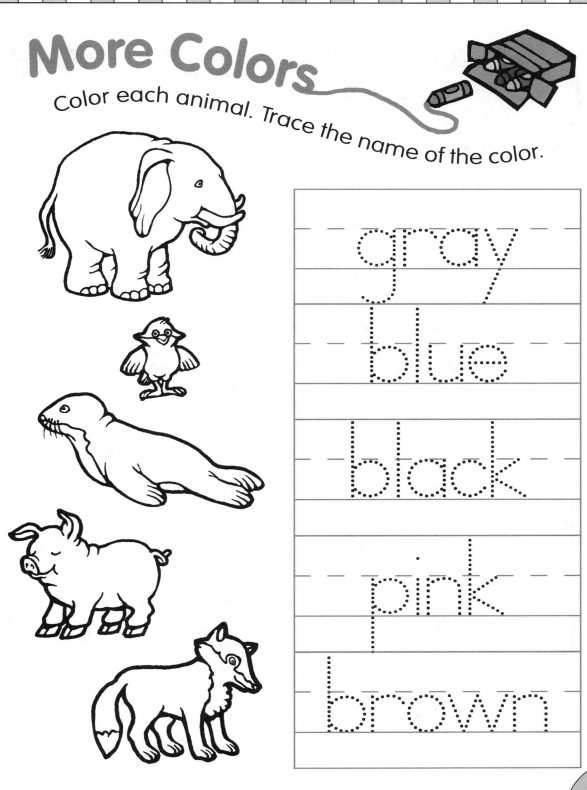

gray

blue

black

pink

brown

Circles

This is a circle. Color all the circles.

Squares

This is a square. Color all the squares.

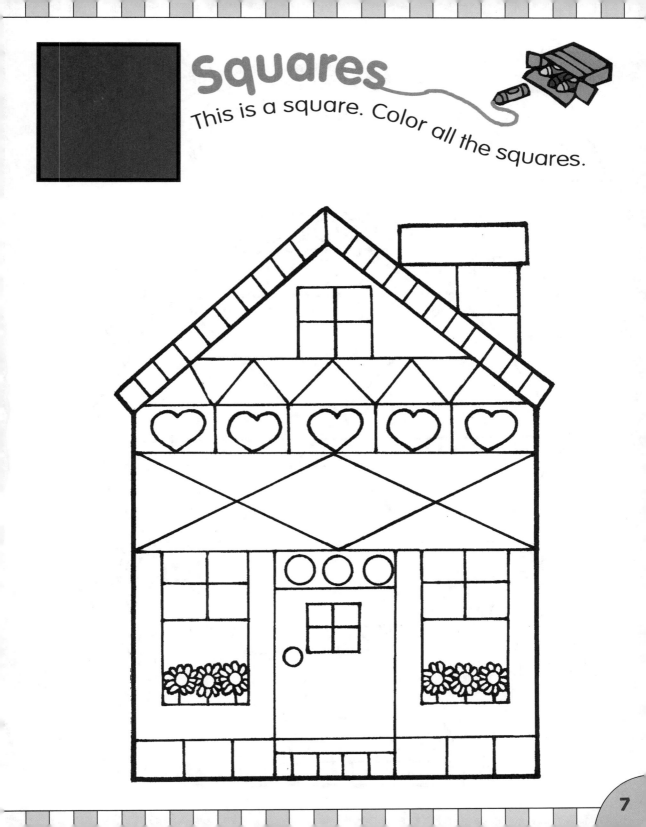

Triangles

This is a triangle. Color all the triangles.

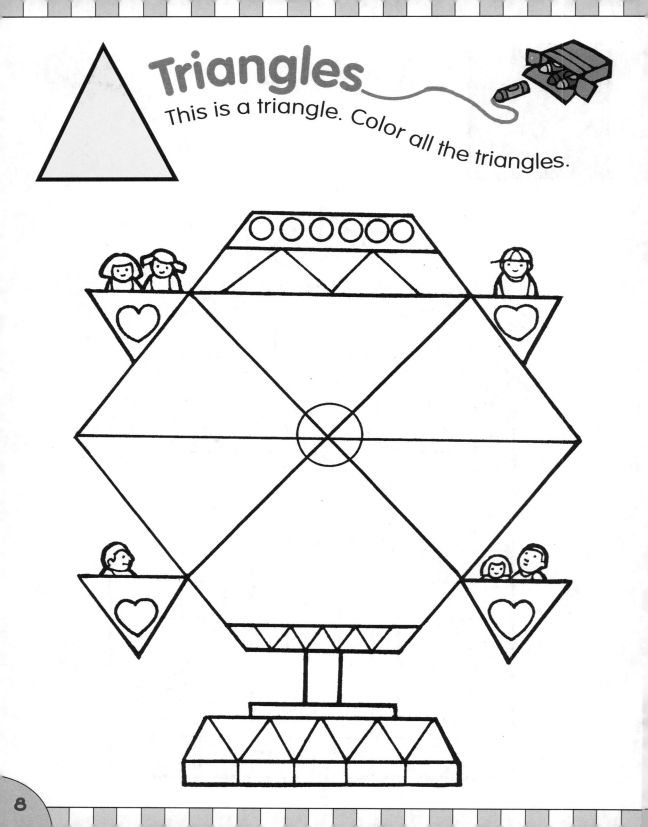

Rectangles

This is a rectangle. Color all the rectangles.

Birthday Shapes

Draw a line between shapes that look the same.

Same Size

Circle the picture that is the same size as the first.

Pick the Shape

Circle the picture that is the same shape as the first.

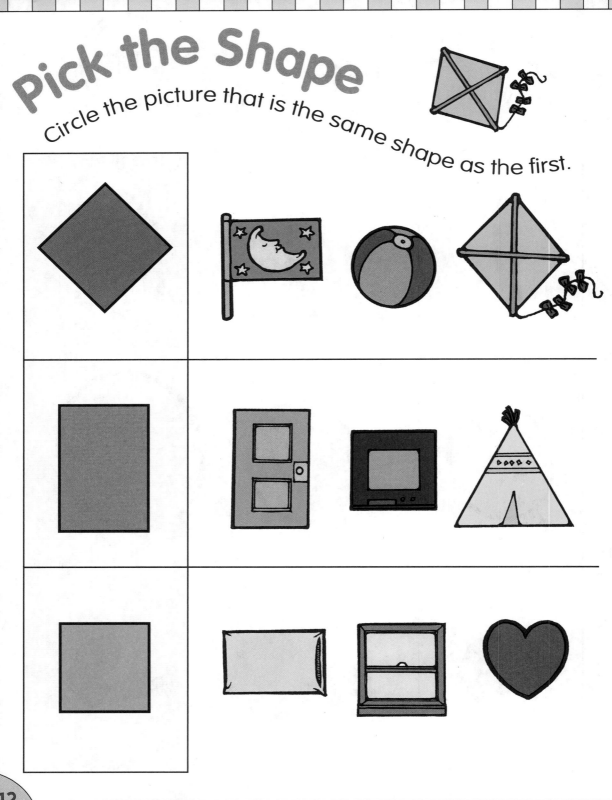

Super Sizes

Draw a line between hearts of the same size.

Beach Shapes

Draw a line between shapes that look the same.

Same Size

Circle the picture that is the same size as the first.

Hidden Shapes

Find and color the hidden circles, rectangles, squares, and triangles.

Shapes Search

Find and color the hidden circles, rectangles, squares, and triangles.

Tickets

What's Next?

Finish the patterns.

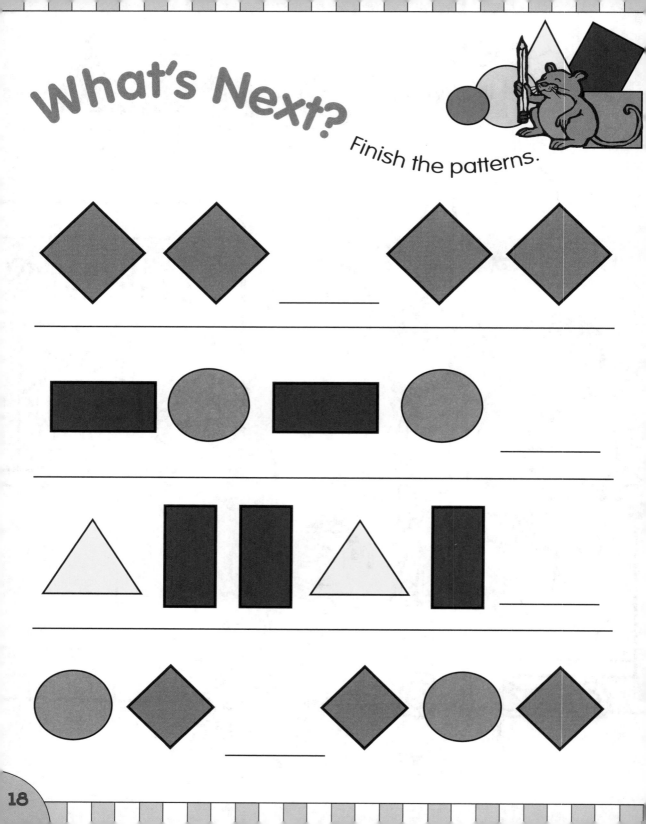

Pretty Patterns

Finish the patterns.

19

More Patterns

20

Make a Face

Finish the patterns.

What Do I Eat?

Draw a line between each animal and its dinner.

Where Do I Live?

Draw a line between each creature and its home.

Make a Match

Draw a line between things that belong together.

More Matches

Draw a line between things that belong together.

What Belongs?

Circle the thing that belongs with the first one.

What a Pair!

Circle the thing that belongs with the first one.

The Same or Different?
Cross out the thing in each row that does not belong.

Which One Doesn't Belong?

Cross out the thing in each row that does not belong.

Fruity Fun

Count the objects. Circle the correct number.

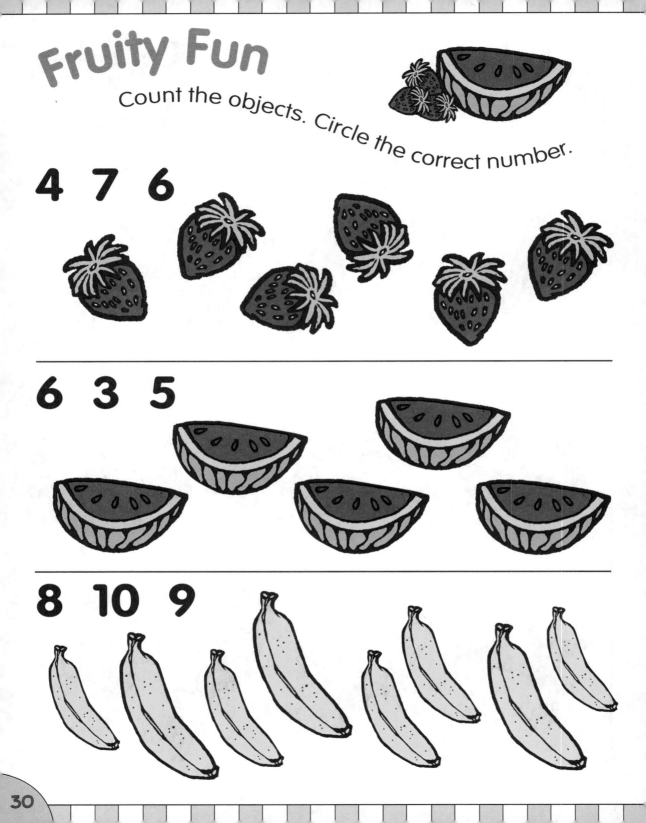

4 7 6

6 3 5

8 10 9

30

Counting Candy

Count the objects. Circle the correct number.

3 2 6

4 5 3

11 8 10

Lots of Toys

Count the objects. Circle the correct number.

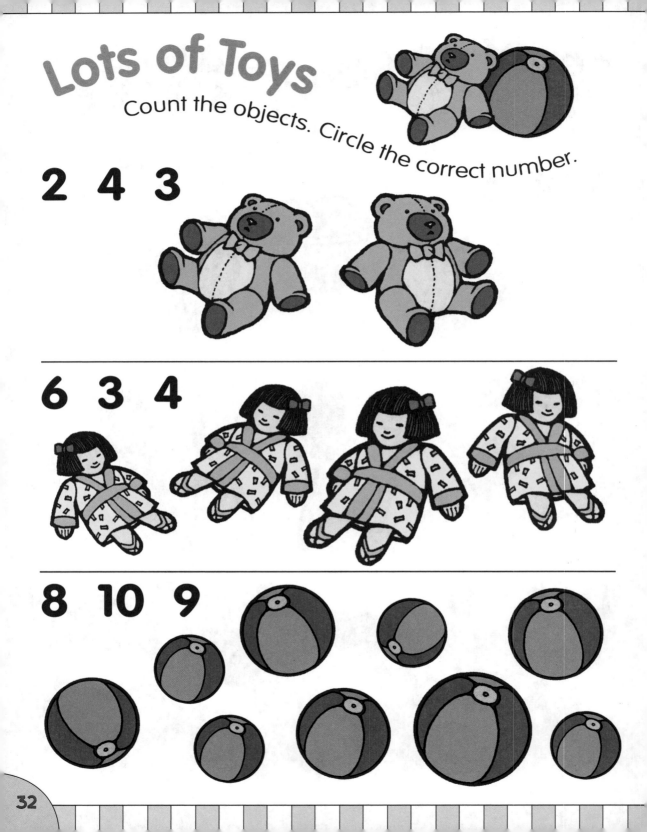

2 4 3

6 3 4

8 10 9

Ready for School

Count the objects. Circle the correct number.

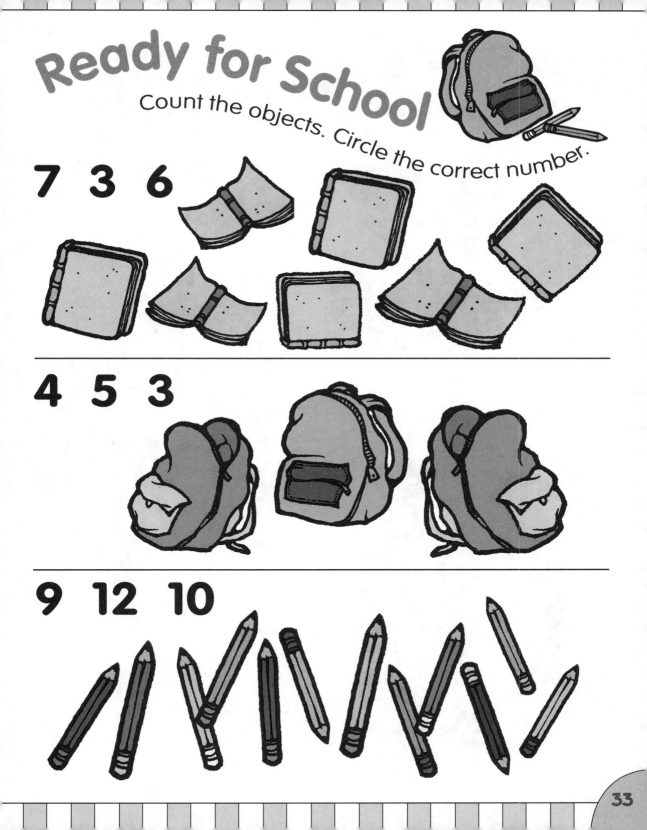

7 3 6

4 5 3

9 12 10

More and More

Circle the group that has more.

More or Less?

Circle the group that has more.

Bunches of Bugs

Circle the group in each row that has less.

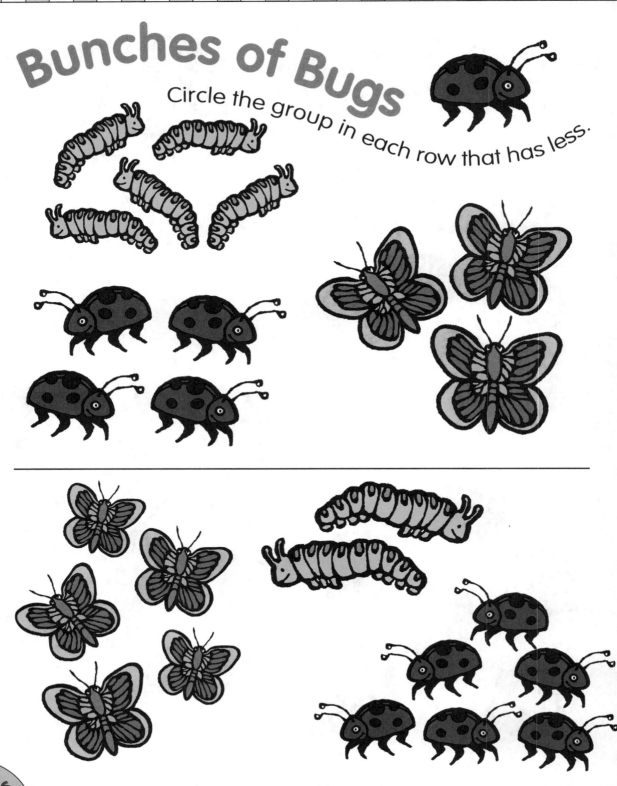

Batches of Buttons
Circle the group in each row that has less.

What Will Happen Next?

Draw a line from each picture to what will happen next.

Guess What's Next!

Draw a line from each picture to what will happen next.

Opposites

Draw a line between each picture and its opposite.

young

happy

big

old

sad

small

More Opposites

Draw a line between each picture and its opposite.

over

up

in

under

down

out

Oodles of Opposites

Draw a line between each picture and its opposite.

neat

dry

cold

messy

wet

hot

42

Different as Day and Night

Draw a line between each picture and its opposite.

night

closed

open

empty

full

day

Time to Rhyme!

Draw a line between words that rhyme.

wig

fox

box

bat

cat

pig

Rhyming Fun

Draw a line between words that rhyme.

truck

bug

rug

duck

can

fan

Find the Rhymes

Draw a line between words that rhyme.

clock

bee

key

toes

nose

sock

Rhyme Wrap Up

Draw a line between words that rhyme.

train

spoon

rake

rain

moon

snake

Listen Carefully

Circle the picture that has the same beginning sound as the first one.

What's That Sound?

Circle the picture that has the same beginning sound as the first one.

Beginning Sounds

Circle the picture that has the same beginning sound as the first one

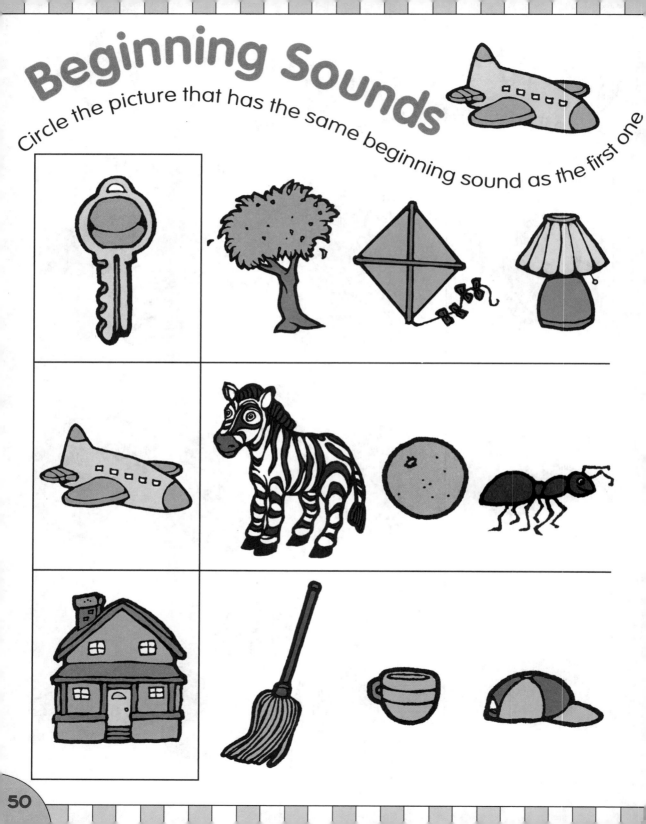

50

More Beginning Sounds

Circle the picture that has the same beginning sound as the first one.

51

The Alphabet

Trace the alphabet.

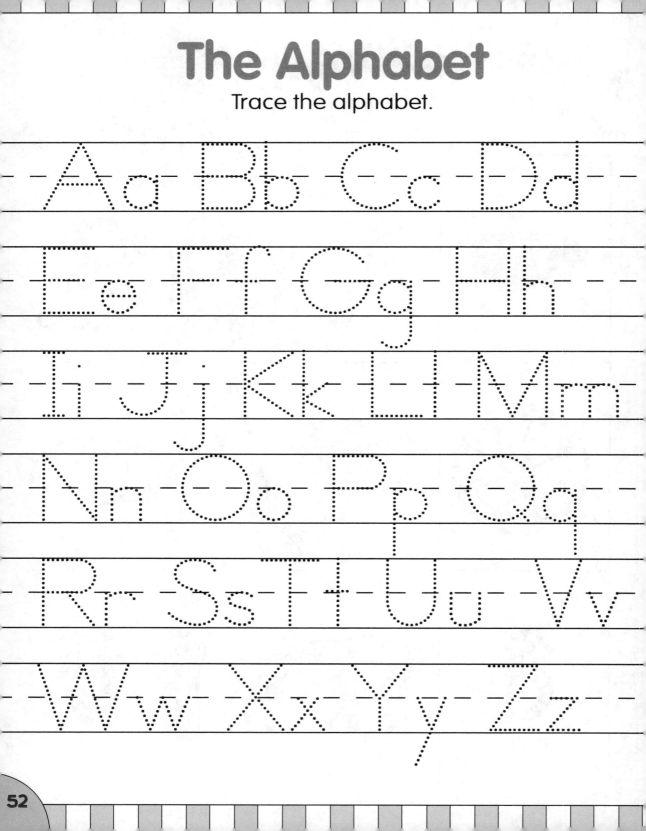

Aa Bb Cc Dd
Ee Ff Gg Hh
Ii Jj Kk Ll Mm
Nn Oo Pp Qq
Rr Ss Tt Uu Vv
Ww Xx Yy Zz

Make a Match

Match each uppercase letter to its lowercase letter.

A

f

B

d

D

a

F

b

53

Big and Little Letters

Match each uppercase letter to its lowercase letter.

Big and Little Letters

Match each uppercase letter to its lowercase letter.

More Big and Little Letters

Match each uppercase letter to its lowercase letter.

Uppercase Letter Match

Circle the letter that is the same as the first one.

M	N K L M
R	C R G D
E	F B E H
Y	I L Y U

Lowercase Letter Match

Circle the letter that is the same as the first one.

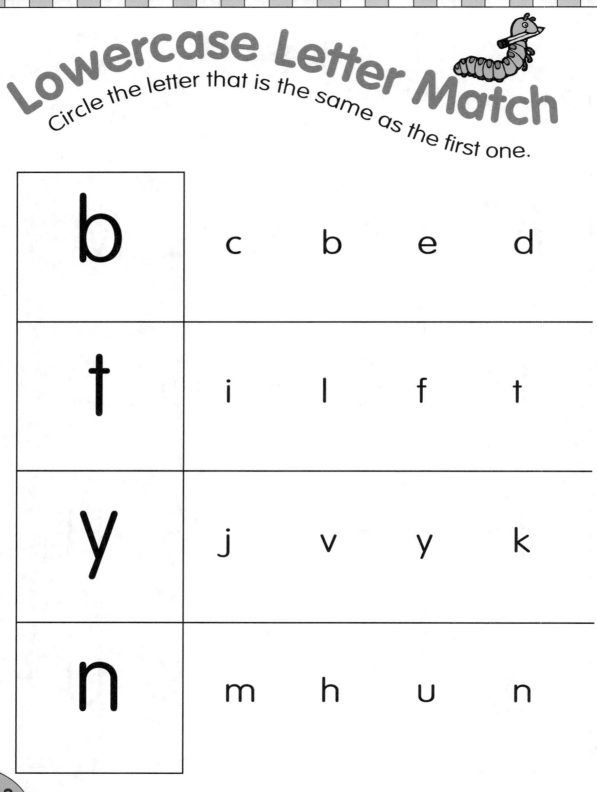

b	c	b	e	d
t	i	l	f	t
y	j	v	y	k
n	m	h	u	n

Word Match

Circle the word that is the same as the first one.

mop   **mop**   mat   map   top

pan   nap   pat   tap   **pan**

cup   pup   cap   cat   **cup**

Animal Word Match

Circle the word that is the same as the first one.

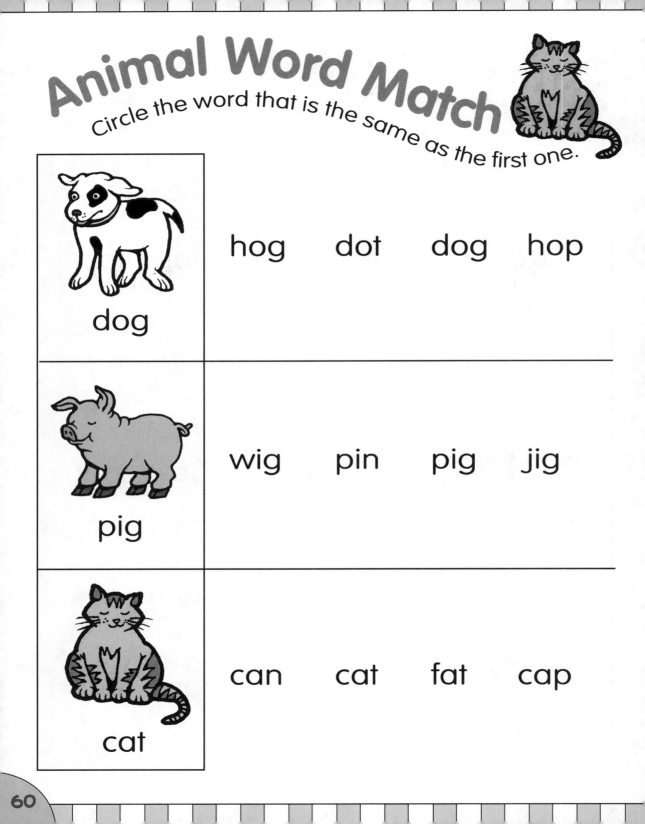

dog	hog dot dog hop
pig	wig pin pig jig
cat	can cat fat cap

Body Word Match

Circle the word that is the same as the first one.

hand	sand land hand and
nose	rose nope close nose
lips	tips list lips slip

Toy Word Match

Circle the word that is the same as the first one.

ball	hall fall bull ball
truck	duck track truck trick
bear	bare bead bear dear

School Word Match

Circle the word that is the same as the first one.

 **desk**	dusk dust desk disk
book	look book took block
bell	ball tell fell bell